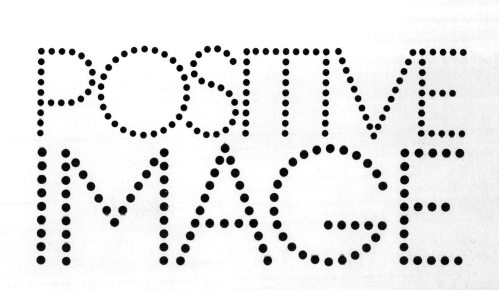

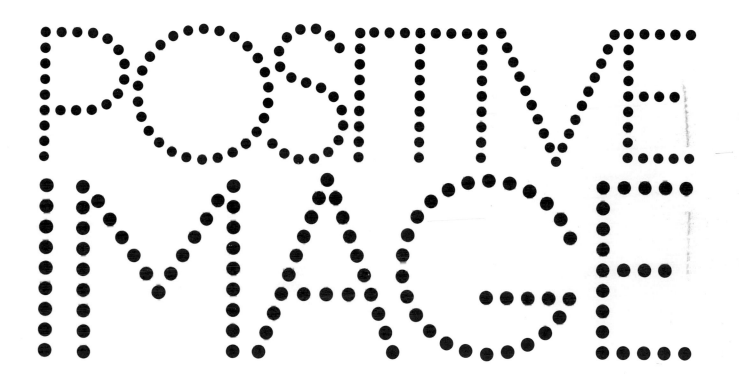

# POSITIVE IMAGE

## A PORTRAIT OF GAY AMERICA BY STEPHEN STEWART

*Text edited by Thomas J. Watson*

William Morrow and Company, Inc. New York

Library of Congress Cataloging in Publication Data

Stewart, Stephen.
   Positive image.

   1. Photography, Documentary—United States.
2. Homosexuals—United States—Pictorial works.
I. Watson, Thomas J. II. Title.
TR820.5.S75   1985      779'.9306766         84-1064
ISBN 0-688-04196-5

Printed in the United States of America


2 3 4 5 6 7 8 9 10

*In memory of my grandmother Sarah Best, who gave me my first camera, along with the courage to see myself and the world through positive eyes*

# INTRODUCTION

The demand that all other people shall resemble ourselves, grows by what it feeds on. If resistance waits till life is reduced nearly to one uniform type, all deviations from that type will come to be considered impious, immoral, even monstrous and contrary to nature. Mankind speedily become unable to conceive diversity, when they have been for some time unaccustomed to see it.

—JOHN STUART MILL
*On Liberty*

**U.S. Army Staff Sergeant Perry Watkins,
Tacoma, Washington**

he birth of Gay Liberation, I sometimes like to argue, occurred in the 1830s with the invention of the camera. If not the birth, then certainly the conception.

Yet only in the past few decades has photography realized its paramount role in creating and capturing a positive image of gay men and lesbians in America. In our visually oriented Western culture, "seeing is believing," and photographs have a unique power to influence the way the world sees us. Still, ultimately more critical is how we come to see ourselves. And what we have begun to see is a new and radical *positive* self-identity, a liberating identity that acknowledges the positive difference we make within the larger society, while celebrating and embracing our individuality.

When the first photographs were taken nearly 150 years ago, extremely long exposures were required. This meant, for example, that a photograph of a busy street would be void of moving objects. The many people on the street became invisible. In time, film speeds increased and exposures decreased. But gay men and lesbians remained invisible for many years to come. Millions of Americans feared and loathed homosexuals they had never seen. In fact, we had rarely seen ourselves. The only thing most of us had in common was our invisibility. By ignoring our existence, non-gay society oppressed us. When we ignored ourselves, often in order to survive, we committed psychological suicide.

Not until the now-legendary gay revolt at the Stonewall Inn in New York's Greenwich Village in 1969 did we begin collectively to see that by remaining invisible we were cooperating with our oppressors and perpetuating our oppression. Overnight, or so it seemed, militant "sissies" became sensational news. We refused to behave according to the image we had been assigned—that of weak and powerless stereotypes. As a result, and much to our advantage, we became "exploited" by the media, and for the first time in American history, homosexuality had a name and a face and could be neatly packaged, labeled, and delivered to the nation's doorstep as "Gay Liberation."

Only six years later, in 1975, Sergeant Leonard Matlovich was photographed for the cover of *Time* magazine. The headline read: I AM A HOMOSEXUAL— THE GAY DRIVE FOR ACCEPTANCE. Matlovich had taken the Air Force to court on grounds of sexual discrimination. The traditionally homophobic military could no longer deny our presence. A larger victory, however, went unnoticed at the time by most: Matlovich's wholesome all-American face and image, if only subconsciously, helped dispel the unspoken myth that all homosexuals are two-headed monsters. More important, he became a role model, an occur-

**Christopher Street subway stop, Greenwich Village, New York**

**A participant in the Fourth Annual West Coast Women's Music and Comedy Festival, Santa Barbara, California, 1983**

rence impossible to imagine just a few years before. Matlovich explained at the time, referring to the New York Gay Pride Rally he had addressed earlier that year: "I found myself, little nobody me, standing up in front of tens of thousands of gay people. And just two years ago I thought I was the only gay in the world. It was a mixture of joy and sadness. It was just great pride to be an American, to know I'm oppressed but able to stand up there and say so."

Two years later, Anita Bryant, a devout member of what may be this country's most homophobic institution, the Church, began her crusade to "Save Our Children" from homosexuals in the name of God. At the height of her "new career," Anita was quoted in *Playboy* magazine: "Homosexuals would have us believe they're born that way, because they're in total darkness and they've never been told any different. But if they're a legitimate minority group, then so are nail biters, dieters, fat people, short people and murderers. Who will be the next in line to ask for special privileges?"

This irrational statement of homophobic resistance was testimony to the power of our recently found visibility to effect change. In a few short years we had gone from obscurity to national attention, in part because of the photographic image.

Ms. Bryant's campaign for non-gay sexual supremacy, however, turned into a Pandora's box of

**Channel 9 News Special: "Is It Safe to Come Out?" Washington, D.C., May 1983**

hype; ironically, it brought real hope to homosexuals, who, in self-defense, united in common cause for dignity and human rights. Anita's persecution inflicted many emotional and physical scars, but in the end, by giving the "Homosexual Enemy" a face—in photograph after photograph—it inadvertently broke down the symbolic closet door for good.

Now, fifteen years after Stonewall, Americans from Tampa, Florida, to Tacoma, Washington, have become almost desensitized by a plethora of magazine and newspaper photographs chronicling "The Gay Movement," "The Gay Lifestyle," and "The Gay Mystique." Susan Sontag, in her book *On Photography*, states: "By getting us used to what, formerly, we could not bear to see or hear, because it was too shocking, painful, or embarrassing, art changes morals—that body of psychic custom and public sanctions that draw a vague boundary between what is emotionally and spontaneously intolerable and what is not."

The power of the documentary photograph to raise social consciousness and to effect positive change is part of an impressive tradition in this country. Most of us first experienced the horrors of war through vivid photographs. We felt "down and out" when we were exposed to the Farm Security Administration documentation of the Great Depression. We were moved perhaps most of all by the powerful images taken at the turn of the century by Lewis Hine. Documenting the desperate conditions of child labor in the mills and factories of a newly industrialized America, he influenced the enactment of child labor laws that reshaped this nation's work force.

Today, gay male and lesbian photographers across the country are enthusiastically exploring, redefining, and documenting who we are . . . and, ultimately, exposing a tragic injustice. Mainstream, non-gay culture has always dominated the image market. Through photographs we can now come to know and identify ourselves, our heroes, our leaders and role models—as well as to celebrate our diversity. When our only images were non-gay, what we saw were gays as distorted as the reflection in a fun-house mirror. This book, then, is both my contribution to our developing positive image and an attempt to shatter a few distorting mirrors and dispel a few remaining superstitions.

*The Random House Dictionary* defines *superstition* as "a belief or notion, not based on reason or knowledge . . . irrational fear of what is unknown."

My definition of superstition is the neighborhood in which I grew up. Living in a typically white, working-class suburb of Los Angeles during the 1950s and 1960s, I was culturally isolated, and presumed that everyone in the world was just like me. And I wanted to believe that I was just like everyone else. I was

**Halloween on Castro Street, San Francisco, 1983**

naïve. I did not find out until college that the boy down the street, Nestle Cohen, was Jewish. Imagine my surprise when I discovered I was gay! No one in my neighborhood was gay—especially in my house. I was not only different, I was now the enemy my family and friends had taught me to fear. There were no gay judges, writers, or football players for me to identify with. Not that they didn't exist—they just weren't visible. They denied their existence as I denied mine. And the irrational fears and myths persisted.

In 1981, ten years after "coming out" in my personal life, I was prepared to come out professionally. As a photographer, I wanted to photograph what I knew best and yet knew nothing about at all. That curiosity led me to this book.

Initially, I set out to take a look at our developing identity—my self-identity. It was not long, however, before I was trying to capture the quintessential "Portrait of the Movement." This attempt didn't last very long; I discovered that there is no comprehensive picture to take! A lesbian does not necessarily see an image the same way a gay man sees it, and even two gay men may see it differently. A gay lobbyist on Capitol Hill probably does not see it the way a female impersonator in Hollywood sees it. And many gay men and lesbians choose not even to look.

**Former home in Chicago of Henry Gerber, co-founder of the earliest-documented homosexual emancipation organization in the United States: the Chicago Society for Human Rights, founded in 1924**

Calvary Cemetery in St. Louis, Missouri, is the site of openly gay playwright Tennessee Williams's unmarked grave. He was buried next to his mother, Edwina Dakin Williams, in February 1983.

Our only commonality appeared to be in our *diversity*, and I did not want to diminish or trivialize that. Non-gay photographers have been doing an excellent job of that on their own. In the tradition of the documentary, I wanted to capture the enormous variety of our lives, even if that variety included images that might be controversial or politically incorrect or difficult to observe. I was not interested in cleaning up our act for the camera, or in rewriting history or our specific heritage. I set out only with the belief that diversity and individuality are beautiful and powerful and positive.

In candid and posed portraits, *Positive Image* attempts to look at the people, places, events, and symbols that have shaped the gay and lesbian image since the turn of the century. I have tried to come face-to-face with the men and women across the country who are affirming their own positive differences in a less than indifferent non-gay society. I wanted to acknowledge the positive differences they are making in all our lives.

Those who agreed to be photographed for this book live open lives and have chosen self-respect above respectability. They are the activists, the artists, the representatives of the minorities within our sexually defined minority. They stand as role models (though not often in the traditional sense), either directly or indirectly, and are responsible for creating the positive impressions that challenge the narrow and oppressive non-gay definition of sexual correctness.

Though I've traveled to many cities in this country, large and small, to parades and rallies, to personal and public events, to homes and offices, I'm certain that I've overlooked gay men and lesbians who have made unique and important contributions to our visibility.

What began as something of a search for my own identity grew into a historical photo-documentation and personal pilgrimage, taking me across the country in a three-year (1982–1984) search for our visual heritage.

Whenever I had the opportunity to explain my project to an individual or group, I received welcome and encouragement. Doors that were ordinarily closed stood open. One of the most gratifying experiences occurred in the summer of 1983, during the preparation for the Fourth Annual West Coast Women's Music and Comedy Festival held in Santa Barbara, California. I was invited by comedienne Robin Tyler to spend a few days with the women who were putting the festival together. I watched them building this "City of Women," as they referred to it, and I felt a special excitement, seeing and recording what few, if any, men have witnessed firsthand. In this event, for women only, I had the rare opportunity to pho-

**The Eighth Annual National Reno Gay Rodeo and County Fair, held in 1983**

tograph lesbians as something of an insider. The result was an intimate portrait, something I had seldom been able to capture before.

Observing the symbols that enforce and create our oppression was another part of my journey. There were many signs and messages along the way, some intentional and some unintentional. The most obvious symbols of oppression were also the most subtle, like the statues and monuments erected to glorify everyone and everything in every city, but never to commemorate acknowledged gay men or lesbians. Many of the monuments, as I looked closely, seemed to offer multiple and often mixed messages—and always revealed more than I suspect they were intended to. When I visited the Iwo Jima monument to the Marines in Arlington, Virginia, years ago, I saw a statue. Returning for a second look in 1983, having learned that the site of the monument had long been a gay cruising area similar to those in other cities across the country, I saw something I hadn't noticed before: an ironic depiction of men thrust together, as if in sexual combat, a visual pun and a new interpretation of the American way of sexual repression and denial.

There were also new symbols of hope. Harvey Fierstein was one. I recall photographing him in his dressing room a few weeks prior to his winning Tony Awards (Best Actor and Best Play) for his Broadway

**Lesbian/feminist Charlotte Bunch, a founder of the Washington, D.C., Women's Liberation Movement, is pictured here in New York Harbor.**

**USA TODAY IS GAY, Charles Street, Boston, Massachusetts, 1983**

play *Torch Song Trilogy*, the moving story of the life and times of a Jewish drag queen. I was certain that Harvey would win, and later, as I watched him accept his awards on national television, I knew that similar accolades belonged to the men and women who had had the courage to come out before there were fashionable discos and Gay Pride parades and before homosexuality was "gay"; to the men and women who paved the way for our acceptance of ourselves and the larger acceptance symbolized by Harvey's awards.

Diane Arbus, who spent many years photographing "freaks," once said, "A photograph is a secret about a secret. The more it tells you the less you know." What she didn't mention is that the picture never taken is the best-kept secret of all.

After making hundreds of prints for this book, I knew that if I didn't know any more about my subject or myself, at the very least I was no longer keeping society's secret. I was no longer behaving as if we didn't exist, or as if our only reason for existing is sexual.

To look at oneself honestly takes courage. We are not the first gay men and lesbians, as someone once remarked—just the first with the opportunity to see and know ourselves honestly. I hope this look at our visual history will encourage us in our continuing efforts to envision a more positive future.

—STEPHEN STEWART
Los Angeles, 1984

he corner of **Christopher and Gay Street is located in the heart of New York City's West Village.** A few blocks down Christopher Street is the site of the old Stonewall Inn, where years of police harassment finally resulted in street fighting and a long-overdue gay rebellion against oppression. Occurring in the summer of 1969, it is regarded today as the birth of the Gay Liberation movement in this country.

In June 1970 the First Annual Christopher Street Liberation Day Parade marched from Greenwich Village to Central Park, with ten thousand people participating. The first Christopher Street/West Parade occurred simultaneously in Los Angeles. Longer marches took place the following year, and today "Gay Lib" is celebrated annually in countries around the world.

The word *gay* is derived from the French term *les gai,* once used to describe men who performed as women on the stage. (Women, for hundreds of years, were not allowed to work in the theater.) When the term arrived in America in the early 1900s, it was picked up and used as a code word in place of the term *homosexual,* which is a clinically defined label with negative connotations. By the late 1960s the word *gay* had become a *symbol* of self-affirmation and an emerging self-definition for the gay and lesbian community.

Today *gay* defines an alternative lifestyle and a minority in which sexual activity is but one aspect.

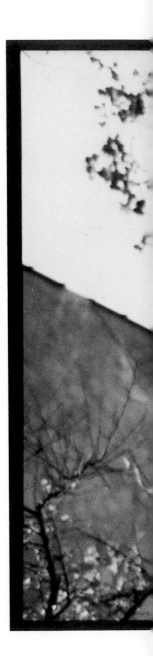

**T**wo, four, six, eight, how do you know your kid is straight?" is a slogan heard at gay rallies and parades around the country.

Slogans originated as battle cries, used by Scottish Highland and Irish clans, and the earliest gay slogans followed in this tradition. "Out of the closet, into the streets" and "Hey, Hey, What do you say? Try it once the other way!" served to excite and motivate our community, reminding us that oppressive myths and stereotypes can be destroyed if we make ourselves visible.

Making themselves visible, gay and proud runners stretch before **Los Angeles' First Annual Run for Gay Pride, held in the Silver Lake area, 1982.**

Most slogans are rallying mottos, designed to sell a product or inspire a crowd. Perhaps the most affirmative gay slogan currently heard—one that sums up what our experience is all about—is "Say it loud, I'm gay and proud!"

What volumes could say it better?

• • • • • • • •'m not willing to change who I am to sell records," says **singer-songwriter Holly Near (photographed here in New York City)**. When she sings, "We are a gentle and angry people, singing for our lives," she alludes not only to the gay community and its struggle for human rights, but to all people concerned about nuclear power, war, feminism, racism, and other humanistic concerns. Her courageous voice thunders across a land where only a decade ago there was deafening silence.

Holly, who once dated men, openly declared herself gay in 1976. She recalled later: "I thought, 'Gosh, can I really deal with what society hands out to a lesbian?' Then I decided that wasn't a fair choice—to deny myself a happy and healthy part of life because of social criticism. . . . I want to do songs about lesbians in such a way that both gay and straight teenagers will ask their parents to come to concerts."

Having founded her own record label—Redwood Records—in 1973, Holly has continued to sing out about the issues and emotions that affect her most. In fact, many of her love songs express the love between two women.

**K**issing booths are an American tradition, and the one at the **Los Angeles Gay Pride Festival, 1982,** was as much a parody of this tradition as it was a celebration of the freedom to be part of it.

Gay Pride parades and festivals are held in June of each year in many cities around the country to commemorate the 1969 Stonewall uprising and the subsequent start of the Gay Liberation movement. They celebrate newly won freedoms that allow gay men and women to participate in activities—including public kissing booths!—so long denied.

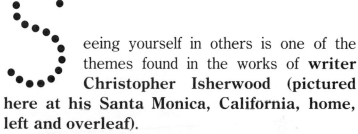eeing yourself in others is one of the themes found in the works of **writer Christopher Isherwood (pictured here at his Santa Monica, California, home, left and overleaf).**

Isherwood is probably best known for his *Berlin Stories* (1946), which became the basis for the play *I Am a Camera* and the hit musical *Cabaret*. In 1976, Christopher published an autobiographical account of his life and gay times in Berlin of the 1930s, under the title *Christopher and His Kind*. In it he describes the initial shock and dismay he felt upon being introduced at the Hirschfeld Institute to homosexuals who had habits and life-styles perhaps more "freakish" than his own:

"Christopher giggled because, at last, he was being brought face to face with his tribe. Up to now, he had behaved as though the tribe didn't exist and Homosexuality were a private way of life discovered by himself and a few friends. He had always known, of course, that this wasn't true. But now he was forced to admit kinship with these freakish fellow tribesmen and their distasteful customs. And he didn't like it. His first reaction was to blame the Institute. He said to himself: How can they take this stuff so SERI-OUSLY?"

Christopher moved to the United States in the 1940s, and for thirty years has shared a home with his companion, artist Don Bachardy. An increasingly visible spokesperson, Christopher has helped many of us come face-to-face with our own "freakish fellow tribesmen."

preading the word—dispelling myths, educating, sharing and recording stories, histories, and struggles—is an important step in the development of any culture or society.

Yet gay literature, as such, has had a rather short life-span. As recently as 1971, author John Murphy lamented: "When a boy is curious about sex, he can get information about every aspect of sexual activity, psychological, biological, or literary-erotic, at his neighborhood drugstore's paperback rack—if he is interested in heterosexuality. . . . If he has homosexual inclinations, the choice of books dealing with *his* sexual concerns are limited."

*Limited* was a bit of an understatement!

Gay books and bookstores have grown rapidly in the past fifteen years, thanks to a heightened gay consciousness. **The Oscar Wilde Memorial Bookshop (page 41), owned and run by Craig**

Rodwell in New York's Greenwich Village, was the country's first lesbian and gay liberation storefront, founded in 1967.

*Lammas*, owned and operated by Mary Farmer (previous page), is a lesbian/feminist bookstore in Washington, D.C.

These shops—plus *Chosen Books* in Detroit, *A Different Light* in Los Angeles, *Glad Day* in Boston, *Unabridged Bookstore* in Chicago, *Wilde & Stein Books* in Houston, *Giovanni's Room* in Philadelphia, *A Brother's Touch* in Minneapolis, *A Different Drummer* in Seattle, and so many more—offer books by and about lesbians and gay men, literature that "dared not speak its name" only a few years ago.

**T**ime magazine, as recently as 1979, reported that despite "new forms of support, gays still feel isolated and persecuted. . . . Even in cities or states that have freedom-of-sex laws, gays are often in danger of losing jobs, or their apartments, if they come out." Indeed, the magazine quoted a prominent urban district attorney who said, "I view the homosexual community as a quiet but suppurating sore on the body politic."

*Community* is used here in the broadest application, to describe most of the estimated 20 million gay men and lesbians in this country alone. But more and more, in cities with growing populations of visible gays, neighborhoods are emerging in which predominantly homosexual men and women live and work and share their lives. These areas are sometimes described as "gay ghettos." In places like the Castro and Valencia areas of San Francisco, Greenwich Village in New York City, Jamaica Plains in Boston, and the North Shore area in Chicago, the safety and security—or illusion of security—of the ghetto is seductive, if not irresistible. These neighborhoods are usually self-sufficient, with gay-run markets and restaurants, banks and bookstores, movie theaters, bars, and baths.

The word *ghetto* is derived from the Italian *borghetto,* a sixteenth-century word used to describe the walled-in part of Venice, the "little boro" to which Jews were relegated and where they were forced to spend their lives. Today our ghettos have only imaginary walls, and they are prisons only to the self-exiled.

**Pictured here are two examples of ghetto street art: a message of freedom, written in cement a few blocks from Castro Street (left); graffiti and the lesbian sign on a wall in Greenwich Village, America's first popular "gay ghetto" (overleaf).**

ecognition is often accompanied by exploitation. A few years ago an advertising agency announced: "Gay men are our business—our only business. . . . Tired of passing up the huge market that created Disco? If so, contact us and get a grip on the gay bucks hidden in America's economic closet."

Gays have become a particularly desirable target audience for many advertisers. Marketing surveys indicate that the typical gay household—with no children to support—has at its disposal a large discretionary income. Because men generally bring home more money than women, the gay male household has recently been besieged by national advertisers.

"Marketers are beginning to exploit what I call gay sensibilities," warns *Advocate* publisher Peter Frisch.

The presence of a mainstream ad in a gay magazine "says a hell of a lot," according to Frisch. "It says [the manufacturer] doesn't care if you're gay, they want your business. On an emotional level, that's crucial." So who, we might ask, is exploiting whom?

Ads on television, in mainstream magazines, and on billboards feature such gay eye-catchers as partially clad Adonises hawking everything from cologne to cigarettes to underwear. **(The photo at right was taken in Times Square, New York.)**

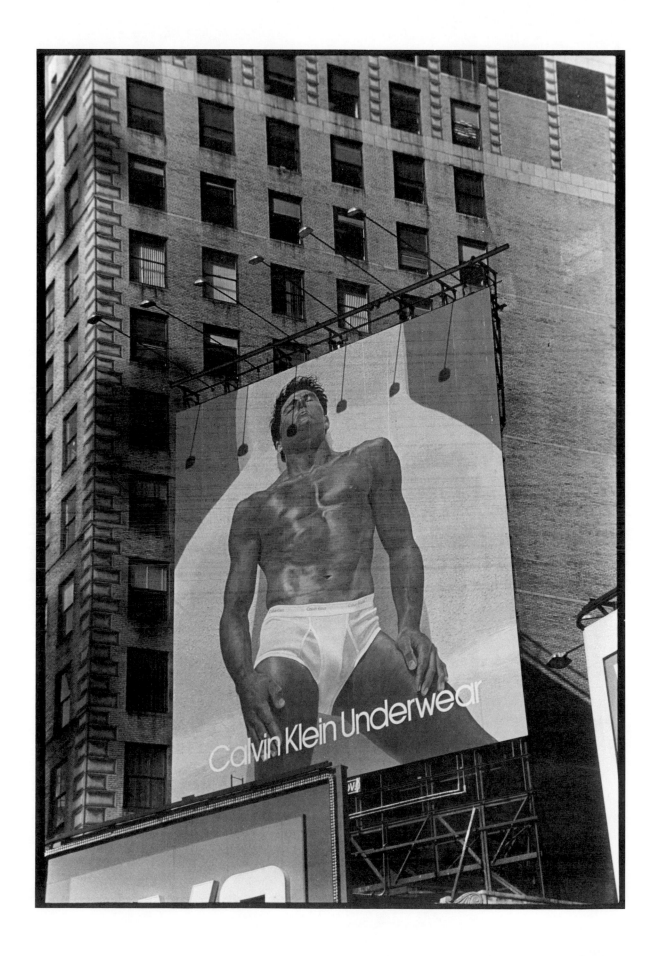

**P**hiladelphia activist **Barbara Gittings (below and at right)** founded the New York chapter of the Daughters of Bilitis—a lesbian organization—in 1958, and in 1965 was a participant in the first picket for gay rights in Philadelphia at Independence Hall. Today Barbara heads the American Library Association's Gay Task Force.

Barbara likes to say that those of us who are fortunate enough to be out of the closet have a responsibility to oil the closet door hinges for those people still unable to come out.

Until the 1960s it was virtually impossible for people like Barbara to find books about gay men and lesbians, except for a few clinical studies of homosexuality. In the past decade, however, gay male and lesbian writers have avidly begun collecting, documenting, researching, and—through the written word—sharing our experiences. According to *The Advocate*, in 1983 there were more than twenty thousand gay and lesbian titles in print.

Individuals like Barbara Gittings have made it possible for lesbians and gay men to find hundreds of books about their life-style, not only in bookstores but in public libraries around the country as well.

50

**U**ntil recently, "drag queens" were the only visible homosexuals in the land. Sensational, campy men in drag tended to attract more media moths to their flame than did men in business suits.

"Since society accords many special benefits to men," Jill Johnston reminds us in *Lesbian Nation*, "it is considered worse for a man to 'act like a woman' than the reverse."

Gay or not, most men still view a man in female drag as an intolerable loss of male prestige and power, while many women and men consider drag to be sexist.

Over the past few years, macho "male drag" has replaced female drag as *de rigueur*, the uniform of the day. And whether these forms of "code dressing" become straight-jackets or liberating forms of expression is limited only by each individual's politics of dress.

**Glenn Scott (photographed, left, in Westwood, and overleaf, in Hollywood, California) does his impression of Marilyn Monroe.** Glenn was born the day Marilyn died and has a special fondness for her. Glenn is comfortable in or out of drag; he lives—and dresses—to his own satisfaction, not to the dictates of others.

Drag queens, however unfashionable at the moment, have earned a special place in our heritage and

a footnote in history: The spark of rebellion that lit the torch of Gay Liberation at the Stonewall Inn, not that many summers ago, came not from boys in boots and jeans, but from the high heels of a few self-respecting men in drag.

**T**he United States military's ban on homosexuals has come into scrutiny many times in recent years, but the case involving **U.S. Army Staff Sergeant Perry Watkins (overleaf, photographed near his home in Tacoma, Washington)** is unique. Appearing on the CBS program *60 Minutes* in January 1983, he discussed his case on one of the nation's most widely viewed shows.

Perry—unlike other people who have challenged the military's right to discharge a person on the basis of sexual preference—openly declared his homosexuality to the Army at the very beginning, in 1968, when he was drafted. They took him anyway, and for fourteen years he served his country well. As one news report verified: "The Army knew he was homosexual but gave him a security clearance to work in a NATO nuclear program. The Army investigated him and found that his homosexuality had never interfered with his or anyone else's duties, and his superiors continually praised his work. He was even hired as a female impersonator to entertain the troops."

But then the Army decided to throw him out—solely because of his sexuality. "The Army did not institute proceedings against me because my homosexuality had created problems," says Perry. "The only reason was because I made the statement that I was homosexual."

Watkins decided to fight back and, in the spring of 1982, took the Army to court. In May of that year, U.S. District Court Judge Barbara J. Rothstein ruled that the Army could not validly discharge Perry on the grounds of homosexuality and, in October, issued a Memorandum Opinion and Order:

"The injury to plaintiff from having relied on the Army's approval of his military career—and being denied it now—is the loss of his career. The harm to the public interest if reenlistment is not prevented is nonexistent. Plaintiff has demonstrated that he is an excellent soldier. His contribution to the Nation's security is of obvious benefit to the public. Furthermore, when the government deals 'carefully, honestly and fairly with its citizens,' the public interest is likewise benefited."

56

56

**S**ecluded in the woods near Santa Barbara, California, totally private, was the **Fourth Annual West Coast Women's Music and Comedy Festival (see overleaf)**. Held over Labor Day weekend, 1983, the festival was created by women, for women. Days and nights were filled with concerts, comedy, crafts, dancing, workshops . . . women's energy . . . women's power.

Perhaps the most important thing the festival provides each year is *space*, space in which the participants can be alone with themselves and with each other. "Women-only space," says the festival brochure, "is an important tradition of women's culture, and a positive affirmation of ourselves."

According to **comedienne Robin Tyler (photographed here with companion Lisa Ulrich at the 1983 festival)**, who has organized the gathering each year: "Women enjoy the safe place of the festival. It is an incredible feeling to realize you are out in the woods with thousands of lesbians who have gone through the same family problems. The Amazon Nation is created. You discover you don't have to hide anymore because all these people are telling you that you're okay."

The festival encourages positiveness rather than negativity. "Our motto," says Robin, "is 'don't criticize, organize.' I tell the women, 'no, you don't get to take something apart in the name of your oppression. You get to contribute.' I don't expect anyone else to pay for my pain, so I don't have to pay for theirs."

Robin, who has two comedy albums of her own in distribution, is pleased by the festival's emphasis on the arts. "You see," she says, "art sustains. We must sing, joke, dance, record, and tape our history. We owe it to our next generation to preserve and support that heritage."

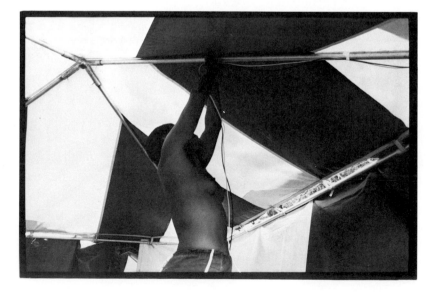

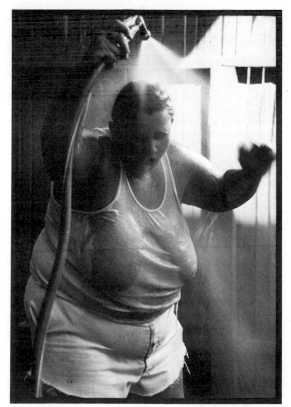

**D**avid B. Goodstein (photographed on his horse, Class to Burn, in Los Angeles) has been an open advocate of gay rights for over thirteen years—since a time in 1970 when he himself was denied a position because of his homosexuality.

"Although I had been actively involved in the civil rights struggles of black people, old people, and Puerto Rican people," he recalled later, "I had never thought seriously about my own civil rights as a gay person. That is, not until that night, the day after I had experienced blatant job discrimination."

From that moment on, Goodstein found himself with a new career: as a full-time volunteer for gay rights. In 1974 he purchased *The Advocate*, a national gay newspaper, and in 1976 helped create the National Gay Rights Lobby. In 1978, Goodstein founded The Advocate Experience, a group-encounter entity independent of the newspaper, designed to offer gays a chance to look at themselves—at cruising, coming out, relationships, family, etc.—in a nonthreatening environment.

Asked about his future as a gay activist, Goodstein has said, "I think the next thing people in the vanguard of the gay movement need to do is take their gayness out into the world. We've already built the foundations of a gay community; now we need to share some of our gay experience with the larger society. The world desperately needs to learn what we can teach it. We need to share our experience of what it means to have sexual freedom."

In his 1983 book, *Superliving*, David explains, "Homosexuality is just one expression of human sexuality, and . . . all people—gay and straight—have to come out of their own particular closet. The world will never be safe for gay people until it is safe for all people to enjoy their sexuality and other human characteristics—both individual and collective. Similarly, white people will never be safe as long as black people are not safe. Christians cannot be free until Jews and Moslems are free."

**A** sign of the times (photo, above) marks the hometown of Reverend Jerry Falwell's Thomas Road Baptist Church and Liberty Baptist College in Lynchburg, Virginia.

Another sign and symbol, ONE WAY (at right), was taken in San Francisco—the "gay mecca" of America.

Conservative politician Barry Goldwater once made it clear that even like-minded individuals do not always agree when giving directions: He exclaimed, "I think every good Christian ought to kick Jerry Falwell's ass."

oming out"—coming to terms with our sexual identity and electing to live an openly gay life—is something we each do at our own pace. Some people, and groups like **the Frontrunners Track Club of Los Angeles (see photo, left)**, "come out running." Others walk, and some people are never able to come out at all.

The area of employment is one in which many live in fear that someday the boss will discover their sexual orientation and end their careers. Few gays and lesbians, even today, know the comfort of working in an accepting and open environment.

"I've never felt better in my life," says Congressman Gerry Studds, who was forced to come out publicly on national television in 1983. "Any person who has ever gone through the experience of coming out will understand that. I feel as if the remaining seven cylinders have just kicked in for the first time in forty-six years—and that's a very powerful feeling."

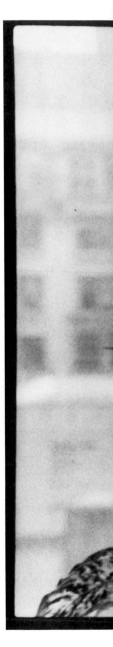

**E**ducating the public—straight and gay alike—is the work and personal goal of **Virginia Apuzzo (right), executive director of the National Gay Task Force and the Fund for Human Dignity, Inc.** "It's time we got the opinion makers to see that we're part of the issues they're championing," she says.

Appointed to head the fund in September 1981, Ginny has been active in the gay movement since the early 1970s. The National Gay Task Force was begun about that time by activist Bruce Voeller and the late Dr. Howard Brown, and others, to provide a professional and national organization for the fledgling gay movement. Voeller became the first executive director, with Jean O'Leary as co-director.

A politician at heart, Virginia Apuzzo points out that openly gay candidates (she ran for the New York State Assembly in 1978) have three major hurdles to overcome: "We have no role models. Our community doesn't take its own candidates seriously enough. And the media refuse to look beyond our sexuality, as if that's all that mattered to us."

Ginny hopes that education will bring about change, but she knows it will not come easy. "Public education is not a quick fix. Public education is not a sprint. It's a marathon. Make a commitment for the long haul, because the opposition is out there, ready, willing, and able to run roughshod over us if we don't make it clear to them that we count. We count. We count to ourselves. We count to each other."

**J**im Kepner, founder and curator of the National Gay Archives—Natalie Barney, Edward Carpenter Library, and a gay activist for thirty years (pictured here in the archives in Los Angeles) has been amassing literature pertaining to gay culture since 1942. His collecting started as a private endeavor, but in 1972 he announced the opening of the Western Gay Archives in his home, allowing people to come in on a part-time basis and make use of his materials. Three years later, by popular demand, the archives opened on a full-time basis. In 1979, the current archive/library institution was established in Hollywood. It houses the largest collection of gay and

lesbian publications in the world, and is used by a wide variety of people and research organizations. Kepner, himself a teacher and author of more than a thousand articles and reviews, says, "I see the archives as having a role not merely of preserving our past heritage, but also defining who and what we are, and what we're good for."

Among the many interesting questions to which one can find answers at the archives is: "for whom was the library named—who were Natalie Barney and Edward Carpenter?"

Natalie Clifford Barney (1876–1972), little known today, was for seventy-five years considered "Empress of the Lesbians" in Paris. A poet, hostess, and American heiress, Ms. Barney's Rue Jacob salon attracted a parade of gay celebrities. An apolitical exemplar of camp life-style, she aided many who were in legal trouble. She and poet Renée Vivien in 1898 urged like-minded women everywhere to help them restore the isle of Lesbos to its ancient glory. Portrayed in *Well of Loneliness, Ladies Almanack,* and in portraits by her lover, Romaine Brooks, she is also remembered for having offended Gertrude Stein, herself a well-known American in Paris, by her open lesbianism.

A pioneer gay liberationist, social critic, mystic, and feminist, Edward Carpenter (1844–1929) resigned as a vicar of the Church of England after being "brought out" by Walt Whitman's verse and ancient Greek sculpture. Later, while working as a gardener and lecturer, he scandalized snobbish friends by having open loving relationships with laborers. His writings on gay themes, especially *Love's Coming of Age, Isolaus, Days with Walt Whitman,* and *The Intermediate Sex,* were major influences before 1950, and his writings on labor and mysticism were equally influential. Not even Oscar Wilde's historic trial deterred Carpenter in his pursuit of broadly defined "gay liberation and spirit."

Opposites in style and philosophy, Natalie Barney and Edward Carpenter both represent major currents in gay history and culture.

ake love, not war!" was a familiar battle cry of the 1960s. Whoever coined this slogan might have been looking at this image of the **Iwo Jima monument** at the time.

In America, it is still acceptable to kill an "enemy" for the love of country, but unacceptable and worse than death for a man sexually to express his love for a fellow countryman.

In 1983, *Social Work* magazine stated, "In an interview, Dr. C. A. Tripp, a researcher at the Kinsey Institute for sex research, associated homosexuality with societies that extol male bravery, courage, and individual derring-do. Such societies idealize masculinity, and thus the easy eroticization of male attributes."

Perhaps the only gay-male cruising or pickup spot that is also a tourist attraction, the Iwo Jima Monument to the Marines in Arlington, Virginia, symbolizes the irony found in sexually rigid societies. Yet, as brave gay men and women continue to battle the rigid intolerance of sexual taboos, love and sex will come out of the bushes, and our society as a whole will be victorious.

**T**here is nothing I need from anyone except love and respect, and anyone who can't give me those two things has no place in my life."

So says Arnold Beckoff, the lead character in the openly gay Broadway play *Torch Song Trilogy.* The words, of course, are those of **playwright-actor Harvey Fierstein (right, in his New York dressing room in 1983**), perhaps the first celebrity in history to thank his gay lover during an acceptance speech on a nationally televised awards show.

Openness and acceptance have always been major themes in Harvey's life and career. He "came out" early in his teens and, like Arnold in *Torch Song,* found work as a drag queen in Greenwich Village. He started dabbling in off-Broadway plays and in 1973, at the age of eighteen, wrote *Flatbush Tosca,* about an Italian drag-queen diva. *Torch Song Trilogy* took three years to prepare, but its immense popularity—not to mention the two Tony Awards it brought its creator—have provided Harvey with professional engagements for years to come. *Torch Song Trilogy* and his book for the 1983 musical version of *La Cage aux Folles* have enriched our lives—and gay culture—immeasurably.

And it all happened without a game plan. Harvey is a living example of being true to oneself and following one's own instincts. "Things happen by accident," he confesses. "They happen because you never say no to life. . . . As long as you don't get scared of living, all the good stuff happens. . . . That's the fabulous part of life: As long as you've got a dream and believe in yourself, you can do it."

arbara Grier and Coletta Reid, in their book *Lesbian Lives*, wrote: "There is as yet no history of lesbian women and how they lived—no record of any particular historical period, ethnic, national or racial group. As far as history is concerned, we are invisible."

Among the people helping to remedy that situation is **lesbian activist Ivy Bottini, pictured here in the Silver Lake area of Los Angeles.** "I knew who I was my whole life," says Ivy, "but for a long time, while married, the mother of two daughters, and living on Long Island, I just didn't know how to get where I wanted to go."

Ivy started to discover how in 1966, when she joined the National Organization for Women (NOW) on the very day that Betty Friedan announced its formation. Ivy, in fact, helped found the first NOW chapter, New York NOW. Lesbianism and its unrecognized role in the struggle for women's rights ultimately cost Ivy her leadership role in this group. As writer Penelope McMillan reported, "Believing that fear of being labeled 'lesbian,' whether true or not, is the ultimate control over women, Ivy organized a panel discussion entitled 'Is Lesbianism a Feminist Issue?' This was the first time lesbianism was openly acknowledged within NOW." From that point on, Ivy admits, lesbianism "could never go back in the closet. People can; the issue can't."

In 1977, Ivy served as director of the Women's Resource Program at Los Angeles' Gay and Lesbian Community Services Center, was Southern California deputy director of the successful "No on Proposition 6" campaign. Proposition 6 was the John Briggs-sponsored anti-gay proposal before the voters in the 1978 elections. She has also served as a member of the Democratic party's State Central Committee, was an open-lesbian appointee of Governor Jerry Brown to the State Commission on Aging, and co-chaired the Lesbian/Gay Caucus of the California Democratic party.

Ivy looks forward to the day when the gay and lesbian community will be able to be self-sufficient in all areas. "I want us to be strong as a community, as a family," she says. "We spend so much time trying to be assimilated; we should start recognizing that we really are like a different race. We have responsibilities to each other. We have to understand that and take care of each other, because the world is not going to do it."

lenn Wein, writing for *Christopher Street* magazine in 1982, recited an all-too-familiar story: "How was I to know that my sixth grade homeroom teacher was a lesbian? If I had known, it would have made my life a hell of a lot easier. Looking back on those years now, I realize that my one big problem was that I couldn't accept the fact that I was a gay kid. I really *knew* I was gay, too. I felt I was different from most of the other boys. I made new problems for myself to take my mind away from what I didn't know how to deal with. I didn't want to deal with being a homosexual because I had been taught that it was a terrible thing to be. Wouldn't my school years have been great if I had been taught how to handle rejection by my peers?"

The first campus gay organization, the Student Homophile League, was formed by a handful of students at New York's Columbia University in the fall of 1966. Gay student unions and support groups have since opened on most college campuses. But what about organizations for youths under college age?

Over the past few years a few organizations have been established to help fill this need. In Massachusetts, for example, **the Boston Alliance of Gay and Lesbian Youth (BAGLY) was founded in 1980. (Pictured here are 1983 president Michael Burnham, right, and fellow-member Stephen Hill.)** BAGLY, whose members range in age from thirteen to twenty-two, meets in a downtown church and provides a variety of discussion groups and social services.

Author Brian McNaught of Boston has written: "A good friend once commented that the most awful thing about being gay is forgetting how awful it was."

houting our love, we have opened many doors and shattered hundreds of years of silence—silence that nurtured intolerance, ignorance, and fear.

Shouting "Liberation" from the rooftop (photo at right, taken in 1982) takes on an added meaning here. This building, the only one remaining of three original structures, housed **the first Gay Community Services Center in Los Angeles.** Founded in 1971, it was the first center of its kind in the country. Located today a few miles away in Hollywood, it is the nation's largest social agency run by and for gay men and lesbians.

In 1983, with a budget of $1.6 million (from both federal funding and private donations) and a paid staff of 45, the center served an average of 7,500 clients per month. Services—many of which are provided free—include health clinics, gay-oriented workshops, legal advice, and youth counseling.

**N**one of us is immune to what others think of us—or how others see us.

In a symbolic gesture, thousands of men and women gathered in West Los Angeles in May 1983 to light the darkness and help us see ourselves, and to help others see us, more clearly. Other similar rallies were held in cities across the country. **The Los Angeles Candlelight Rally (see cover photo, and those at right and overleaf)** was held to attract public attention and funding for determining the cause and combating the spread of AIDS, acquired immune deficiency syndrome.

Between 1980 and early 1984, nearly 3,500 cases of AIDS were reported in the United States—71 percent of them in gay males. An average AIDS patient was expected to live no more than three years after diagnosis.

Yet in this time of crisis, a true spirit of unity, support, and community has shone brightly for many. As Richard Berg, a thirty-eight-year-old AIDS patient in Los Angeles, explained, "Oddly enough, until my AIDS situation actually occurred, I never really identified myself as being part of the gay community. I lived a rather quiet, private life. But my illness brought me into contact with a myriad of loving individuals, each trying to see me through this trying period."

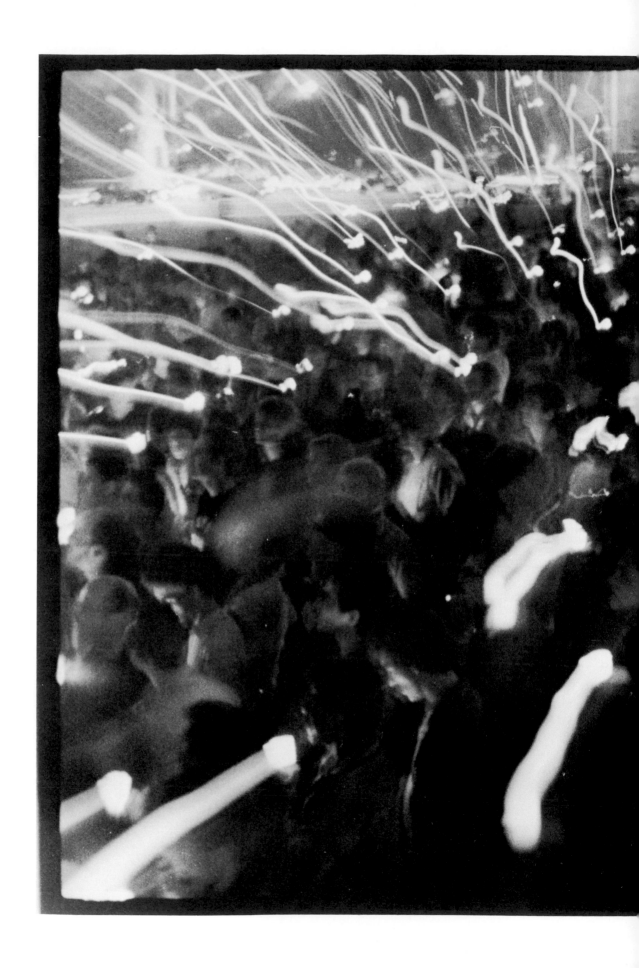

ay parades, such as **the Gay Pride Parade, 1983, held in Los Angeles** (**see photo**), do nothing if not celebrate diversity. As author-critic-Episcopal priest Malcolm Boyd points out, "Diversity is particularly important in gay life because it stands in stark contrast to the conformity that was long forced upon us. So, tolerance for diversity within our community is a high priority.

"We're different—from others, also from one another. . . . Let no would-be dictator try to oversimplify our diversity in the telling, reduce its complexity to an easy formula, cheaply propagandize it, deny it depth, trivialize its tragedy, degrade its joy. . . . Let's be proud of each other as *gays and lesbians* struggling realistically and creatively for strong identity, a maximum of self-esteem, a needed support system within our community, and the redefinition of public images of who we are.

"Give thanks for our diversity. . . . We need each other."

ongtime **Los Angeles gay activist Morris Kight** is regarded by most as the patriarch of the local gay and lesbian community. Morris has championed human rights since the 1930s, and in 1969 he founded the Gay Liberation Front of Los Angeles.

An organizer of and participant in the earliest street demonstrations in 1970, he assisted in establishing Christopher Street West, the first public commemoration of the Stonewall uprising in New York.

One of the founders of the historic Los Angeles Gay Community Services Center, Morris is also a founder of the Stonewall Democratic Club and is an active voice within many other civil and human rights organizations. Here, Morris, in a rare moment of repose, stands before the back door of a local gay bar, which appears to symbolize the bars that have on occasion confined his spirited civil disobedience.

## IMRU

No, it's not a greeting from outer space, but it might as well be part of an alien language. It's the title of a Los Angeles-based gay radio program, pronounced "I am, are you?"

Gay radio has come a long way since 1958, when station KPFA, Berkeley, California, outraged the Federal Communications Commission by including in a live program entitled "The Homosexual in Our Society" statements by psychologists that homosexuality is not an illness.

Today, KPFA has sister stations in Los Angeles, Houston, Washington, D.C., and New York, all of which carry programs with gay and lesbian themes. There is also a San Francisco-based National Gay Network (NGN), as well as Intergay out of New York City, which provide newscasts targeted to the gay community. Both services have subscriber stations in many U.S. cities, in Europe, and in Australia.

David Wynyard, producer of *The Weekly Report from Intergay,* boasts that these radio newscasts can be listened to privately and for free. "We're educating

people, straight and gay, who would not pick up or buy a gay paper."

News, of course, is only one type of gay-theme program available. *Fruit Punch,* the nation's longest-running gay radio program, includes everything from political commentary to presentations of the arts. Originating from KPFA, the series began its broadcasts in June 1973.

**Breakthrough, a weekly lesbian-feminist program from station KPFT, Houston, is co-hosted by activist Pokey Anderson (photographed here in Houston).** Pokey, who co-founded the Houston Gay Political Caucus in 1975 and has been a producer of lesbian cultural events since 1981, finds the power of gay radio particularly effective.

Greg Gordon, executive producer of *imru* agrees: "We have no way of knowing what percentage of our audience is closeted or out, gay or straight. We try to program to the widest spectrum. But it's clear from the letters we receive that for many listeners we are often their only link to the gay community."

**W**ashington, D.C., our nation's capital, has often turned a deaf ear to the needs and rights of homosexuals. For years it has governed the land of the free and the home of the straight.

Gradually, however, the gay community has been making its presence felt in Washington. In 1979, for example, between fifty thousand and one hundred thousand people from nearly every state in the union gathered there to demand civil rights protection for gays and lesbians. As one wire service reported, "Most marchers were young, white and male, but the throng included lesbians, gay men of all ages, and a few mothers pushing or carrying their babies. . . . They marched down Pennsylvania Avenue and behind the White House, then gathered on the Mall below the Washington Monument to hear dozens of speakers denounce what one called the 'homophobia' and 'heterosexism' of mainstream Americans."

Representing gay interests in the nation's capital for many years was **Steve Endean (pictured here near the Washington Monument), until 1983 the head of the Gay Rights National Lobby.** A native of Bloomington, Minnesota, Steve has been active politically since the age of eighteen. He once hoped to run for public office, and knowing what being gay would mean politically, he hid his inclinations— even from himself.

Life proved to be a "nightmare," and in 1970, at the age of twenty-two, Steve came out.

"I knew when I came out I closed a lot of doors to political office, or thought I had," he said later. "It was a hell of a choice."

Steve's work in Washington as a lobbyist was aimed at winning acceptance for gays not only on the streets, but in jobs, housing, and, yes, public office. "The fact that that was closed to me is maybe part of my drive . . . to try to make life better, so the next group of gay people don't have to go through the same painful disappointments."

ur new openness and freedom to express our sexuality manifests itself in symbolic acts that are often more humorous and playful than profound.

*Webster's Dictionary* defines *symbol* as "an act, sound, or material object having cultural significance and the capacity to excite or objectify a response."

In Hollywood, little is left to the imagination. Where and how we live become status symbols, and our cars tend to reflect our life-style most of all. Transportation takes a backseat to the statements we make with our personalized license plates. **"Beefcake" (see photo)** is the gay males' answer to the traditional "cheesecake"—sexy female pinups, centerfolds, and beauty contests (see photo overleaf).

**W**hether regarded as sexy or sexist, the freedom to celebrate the full range of sexuality and self-expression is the ultimate reward of gay liberation.

**The Seventh Annual Mr. Gay California Contest**, which selected a finalist for the 1983 Mr. Gay USA Contest, is one of the many events that symbolize and celebrate this newfound freedom.

A beautiful body has the power to "excite or objectify a response." It is doubtful that Walt Whitman could have anticipated a contest like that held in San Diego when he wrote: "There was a child went forth every day, and the first object he look'd upon, that object he became, and that object became a part of him for the day or a certain part of the day, or for many years or stretching cycles of years."

Yet, without a doubt, Whitman saw something then that still applies today: that all development and growth takes place in stages—and sometimes even on a stage.

**G**od did not create Adam and Steve, but Adam and Eve," said the Reverend Jerry Falwell during his protest of the Gay March on Washington in 1979. Homosexuality, he stated, is "an outright assault on the family."

Statistics estimate that 10 percent of the world's population is homosexual, approximately one child in every four families. Social studies further tell us that while the traditional nuclear family of which Reverend Falwell speaks is, indeed, on the decline, the idea of family unity—familial bonding—has never been stronger. What *is* changing, of course, is the demographic composition of the individual units.

Non-gays and gays alike are changing the definition of the word *family*. Single men and women of any sexual persuasion are choosing to live together, or live alone, with or without the company of children. Many lesbians are chosing to be mothers, and some openly gay men have been able to adopt children. Many people have married, had children, and *then* come to confront their own homosexuality.

One now-divorced gay father recently wrote that he wants his son "to grow up knowing his father and some uncles are gay and to understand them as people and not the shadowy freaks they have been falsely portrayed to be. . . . I have no fear of my son being gay. . . . Whether my son is gay or heterosexual or somewhere in between I will not honestly care. I just want him to be happy as the person he is and to know he had the support of his family."

Unfortunately, not all gay mothers and fathers are as lucky as this man. Many are denied custody of their children. One man recently lamented, "Joint custody is very common in California, but the term 'gay parent' is synonomous with 'unfit parent.'"

**Photographed together in Massachusetts, gay brother and sister Armando and Hortensia Amaro** are typical of many families in which more than one member is gay. Gay siblings have always been part of the family, but only today is it possible for them to share this extra bond in the fullest and truest sense of brother-and-sisterhood.

●
●
●
●
●
●
●
●

t has often been said, and Jean O'Leary has said it often: "If we were all to turn lavender tomorrow, there would be a lot of shocked faces, and also a lot of power right there."

**Jean O'Leary (photographed on the Los Angeles City Hall Mall) is the executive director of the National Gay Rights Advocates,** a gay public-interest law firm that handles precedent-setting cases involving gay people. She is the former co-executive director of the National Gay Task Force, the country's largest gay organization, and the past president of the National Association of Business Councils, a gay business organization with business guilds in twenty U.S. cities.

Jean presently serves on the executive committee of the Gay Rights National Lobby. She has also been a delegate to the last two Democratic conventions, was the first openly gay person to serve on a presidential commission, and was responsible for organizing the first meeting of gay people in the White House in 1976.

Ms. O'Leary has more than fourteen years of national gay rights work experience and is considered one of the most prominent gay people in the country.

n 1968, Dignity, an organization for gay and lesbian Catholics, was founded.

The same year, **Reverend Troy Perry (pictured below)**, author of *The Lord Is My Shepherd and He Knows I'm Gay,* founded the Universal Fellowship of Metropolitan Community Churches. Within ten years, MCC had grown to include 121 meeting groups (including chartered

churches, missions, and study groups) in thirty-one states and seven countries.

The temple Beth Chayim Chadshim ("House of New Life"), the first predominantly gay synagogue in the history of Judaism, was founded in Los Angeles in 1973. Sister temples have since opened in San Francisco, New York, and Miami.

While alternative churches now embrace nearly every conceivable form of worship in this country, hostility and prejudice persist among many organized religions (see the photo sequence at left, taken during the **1983 Gay Pride Parade in Los Angeles).**

An advertisement in 1980 for a KABC-TV (Los Angeles) *Eyewitness News Special Report,* "How to Hurt a Gay Without Even Trying," included the following advice:

"Just close your eyes. And pretend all the gays will go away. . . . Even though they've been a part of society since the beginning of recorded history, you don't have to learn a thing about what they're really like. . . . And you don't have to watch our *Eyewitness News Closeup,* "The Gay 80's," either. . . . See how easy it is to hurt a gay? . . . On the mere chance, however, that you're willing to shatter a few stereotypes, we urge you to tune in this compelling report with psychiatrist Dr. William Rader. . . . It's more than likely that someone you know and love—a friend, a work associate, or even a relative—is gay. And that's where Dr. Rader can help. Because it's what you don't know that can hurt the most."

What people know and don't know today is due in large measure to what is—or what is not—presented by the electronic media. "Let's face it," says Neil Elliot, chairman of the board of directors for Los Angeles' Alliance for Gay Artists in the Entertainment Industry, "television is the most powerful instrument in the history of humanity. Add movies and theatre, and you've got an enormous force for social change—or a monstrous perpetrator of misinformation. Providing viewers with accurate depictions of gays and lesbians is the single most important step to making homosexuality widely understood and accepted." The variety of photos on the following pages and at left illustrates just some of the air time devoted to gay themes on television during recent years: **(Left) a WDVM-TV (Washington, D.C.)** *Eyewitness News Special Report,* **1983, asked the question "Is It Safe to Come Out?"** and reported on our growing visibility and acceptance in the District of Columbia—and nationwide.

**(Overleaf, left to right): 1. KTLA-TV (Los Angeles) News coverage of the January 6, 1984, public outcry over the release of Dan White from Soledad State Prison** after he had served only a five-year sentence for the murders of San Francisco Mayor George Moscone and gay Supervisor Harvey Milk.

2. **Lance Loud,** who came out at age twenty-one on the highly acclaimed 1973 PBS documentary series *An American Family.*

3. **ABC-TV** *20/20* **news magazine coverage of "AIDS: An Epidemic Loose in America,"** one of the first in-depth looks at AIDS, airing many months after medical science had identified acquired immune deficiency syndrome, and after hundreds of affected patients had died.

4. **KNXT-TV (Los Angeles) coverage of gay churches.**

5. **KNXT-TV (Los Angeles) coverage of the gay community.**

6. and 7. **Playwright-actor Harvey Fierstein** accepting two Tony Awards for his Broadway play *Torch Song Trilogy.*

8. **KNXT-TV (Los Angeles) interview with Jerry Falwell.**

9. and 10. **ABC-TV daytime drama** *All My Children* introduced in 1983 a sensitive and sympathetic character, Lynn (played by actress Donna Pescow), who just happened to be a lesbian—an unprecedented occurrence on daytime television.

11. **KABC-TV (Los Angeles), Dr. William Rader reports on the AIDS crisis.**

12. **KTLA-TV (Los Angeles) news coverage mentioning the late Supervisor Harvey Milk.**

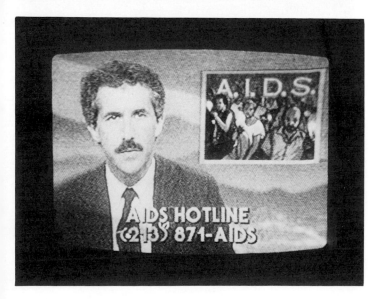

**B**oston gay activist Brian McNaught (photographed here before City Hall) has been involved full time with the gay rights movement since 1974. Most recently he served as Mayor Kevin White's liaison to Boston's gay and lesbian community. He is also the founder of the Detroit chapter of Dignity, a national organization for gay Catholics.

An award-winning writer, Brian is the author of a regularly syndicated column, "A Disturbed Peace," which has appeared in various gay-oriented community papers around the country since 1975. Other articles have appeared in mainstream newspapers and magazines in Houston, Pittsburgh, Cleveland, Milwaukee, Detroit, Miami, Philadelphia, Boston, San Diego, and Washington, D.C.

A collection of Brian's essays was published in 1981 in a volume also titled *A Disturbed Peace.* In one essay he writes, "More than any other generation of homosexuals in the history of the world, we have the opportunity to make things a lot easier for those who follow us. More than the opportunity, we have the responsibility. Few persons will be aware of our struggle 50 years from now any more than we can imagine life without electricity. But the simple knowledge that the little ones who grow up knowing they're gay won't be forced to hide their light under a bushel should be enough cause for celebration today."

he book *Lesbian Lives*, edited by Barbara Grier and Coletta Reid, points out the importance of history to the gay and lesbian movement. It says: "The hushing up of who we have been leaves us no history of ourselves as a people. We don't know who our heroines were, who of us rebelled in spectacular ways, who lived in long, fruitful relationships. We have no role models to point to, no one to learn from."

Two women we might all learn from are **Phyllis Lyon and Del Martin.** Dedicated to the right of the individual to live a life of his or her own choosing, Phyllis (left) and Del (right) pose here before a stone wall **in San Francisco**. This wall symbolizes the many "stone walls" that have obstructed—but never deterred them in their struggle for gay and lesbian rights.

Phyllis and Del have been living together as a couple for more than thirty years. Pioneers in the lesbian, gay, and women's movements, they co-founded in 1955 what is recognized as the oldest lesbian organization in America, the Daughters of Bilitis.

Today, both women are government officials: Phyllis serves as chairperson of San Francisco's Human Rights Commission, and Del is a member of the California State Commission on Crime Control and Violence Prevention.

In their book, *Lesbian/Woman*, first published in 1972 and now in its fifth printing, Phyllis and Del write, "Behind that simple statement, 'I am a lesbian,' are implications so vast that the individual who would survive with any measure of sanity must examine all that she has ever been taught, all that she has ever experienced, all that she has ever hoped or dreamed. Some never make it through this long and lonely journey. They can't face rejection, the concept of being 'queer' or different. They believe the myths and accept what they see on the surface of gay life."

**P**art of defining ourselves is the creation of a common language—oral, written, and visual," says photographer Joan E. Biren ("JEB"). "Without a visual identity, we have no community, no support network, no movement. Making oneself visible is a political act."

JEB is known and respected for helping create that "visual identity," by capturing in photographs the realities of the lesbian experience in America.

One of her contemporaries in the photographic profession is **Arthur Tress (above and right)**, a New York photographer who is recognized the world over for his visual studies of male-identified symbols and other decidedly gay male fantasies.

"What my photographs are *about*," he says, "and what I think homosexuality is for me and for male sexuality in general, is power—power relationships and power exploitation in both negative and positive ways."

**A**sian-American radical Merle Woo made headlines during the early 1980s when she was fired from her job as lecturer in Asian American Studies (AAS), University of California, Berkeley. Her dismissal was linked not only to her criticism of conservative policies in AAS—the elimination of student democracy, community-related courses, and the goal of a Third World College—but also to her militant outspokenness as a socialist-feminist lesbian and trade unionist.

Merle, a member of Radical Women and the Freedom Socialist Party, is pictured in front of their offices in San Francisco.

A veteran lecturer for thirteen years, Merle is not reticent about speaking her mind regarding issues affecting her very existence. "I criticized and made statements about who I am, fully and with dignity. I took my free speech rights seriously, knowing that if I fought back, I was fighting for us all. I grew up in a capitalist society, never hearing about Third World people, women, lesbians and gays—our history of resistance, of culture and art. We will no longer be censored. Moreover, I believe that we must not only continually struggle to preserve hard-won civil rights as oppressed peoples, but also strive to build a socialist society where all freedoms will be realized."

Woo and her Defense Committee waged a two-year legal battle against the University of California, charging violation of her First Amendment rights and discrimination based on race, sex, sexuality, and political ideology. On February 17, 1984, she won a settlement from UC of two years' reinstatement and $73,584.

ith only twelve notes to a musical scale, limitless numbers of beautiful compositions have been created.

The same is true, of course, of people. There are only two basic types of human beings, and yet the variety of possible relationships are many.

Photographed during rehearsals, **the Windy City Gay Chorus,** founded in 1979, proves that there is more than one song and more than one way to sing it—and that there definitely is music after disco.

Gay choruses are heard all around the country today. In Chicago alone, it is possible to listen to the Windy City Gay Chorus; the Artemis Singers, a woman's group; and the Chicago Gay Men's Chorus.

"K ill a Queer for Christ" was a bumper-sticker slogan that reflected a popular sentiment in **Dade County, Florida,** in 1977, during Anita Bryant's crusade to "Save Our Children" from the perversions of homosexuality.

Launching a campaign to repeal an ordinance banning discrimination against gays in employment, she single-handedly brought a local issue to national attention. Her crusade brought hurt to many, yet in a very backhanded way did do some good for the gay community: She forced the nation to acknowledge us! By the time the controversy had ended, every American had to face the fact that gays exist. The purported 20 million gays in the United States could never be ignored again.

Masters and Johnson, referring to the public's misconceptions about gays, have said, "People who stop and think will say, hey, these are somebody's brothers and sisters, wives and husbands, sons and daughters, friends and neighbors, and they are loved and loving human beings."

In Dade County today, bumper stickers are more likely to reflect messages of love than hate (see photo at right, taken in Coconut Grove, Florida). More and more, people are putting on the brakes of public misconception and "stopping to think."

**R**and Schrader (pictured here in his court chambers), an openly gay activist and champion of gay rights for the past fifteen years, was in 1980 appointed judge of the municipal court of Los Angeles by Governor Jerry Brown.

Such appointments are vitally important to the gay community, for, as Harvey Milk explained, "Like every other group, we must be judged by our leaders and by those who are themselves gay, those who are visible. For invisible, we remain in limbo—a myth, a person with no parents, no brothers, no sisters, no friends who are straight, no important positions in employment. A gay person in office can set a tone, can command respect not only from the larger community, but from the young people in our own community who need both examples and hope."

**F**rom New York's Fire Island to California's Russian River, from Provincetown, Massachusetts, to Key West, Florida, gay and lesbian resorts provide us with a refuge from an often still-intolerant society.

Jill Johnston, in *Lesbian Nation*, wrote, "If you can't walk out of your door and down the street and into the park in any familiar embrace with the one you love, the whole society is in trouble."

The freedoms of which Jill speaks are available to many gays only at **resorts (see photos: Provincetown and Cape Cod beach, above right and overleaf; Coconut Grove, Florida, below right).** These locales were at one time carefully guarded secrets, known to only a select few. "Hideaways," they were called—for obvious reasons. Today these resorts are well publicized in the gay press, and have become meccas for freedom-loving homosexuals who, for at least a week or two a year, can feel safe embracing their true selves.

**D**ykes on Bikes"—that's how a group of women who ride each year in the **Los Angeles Gay Pride Parade (photo, left, 1983)** describe themselves.

The once-derogatory term *dyke* has taken on new connotations for many lesbians: strength, defiance, self-affirmation. They wear the name proudly.

"Visibility," says author Don Shewey in *Lavender Culture,* "is the best tool we have to get rid of fears, myths, and misconceptions about homosexuality. And an unsympathetic or unrepresentative portrait of gay people can often be as beneficial as the most sensitive one if it succeeds in opening up a dialogue."

**W**hile acceptance and understanding of individual differences grow out of community sharing at festivals like the annual **Sunset Junction Gay and Lesbian Street Fair (memorialized in this street mural, photographed in Los Angeles' Silver Lake area),** prejudice persists in other neighborhoods, community festivals, and entertainment centers.

In 1980, nineteen-year-old Andrew Exler and his seventeen-year-old companion were removed from a Disneyland dance floor and escorted out of the park when they attempted to dance together during Date Night. According to Exler, the security guards stated: "This is a family park—there's no room for alternative life-styles. Two men can't dance together. This is our policy."

Intolerance thus continues to be an accepted reality, while love remains frightening in America's Fantasyland.

To come out of the closet in a large melting-pot city like San Francisco or New York, and to march in a parade of 300,000, is still difficult for many lesbians and gay men. To come out and march in a parade of 300, down a street in America's conservative heartland, takes a special brand of courage.

That bravery—that conviction—is what Missourians witnessed for the first time in 1979, when the city of St. Louis held its first Gay Pride Celebration Week. Organized by Jim Thomas, founder of the city's *Gay News-Telegraph* and coordinator for the Gay March on Washington in 1979, three hundred men and women marched down Lindel Boulevard, making a statement about themselves and for those who, for various reasons, did not dare to join in.

Such courage requires a great deal of support, and one group that is providing support and counseling for gay communities like that in St. Louis is the National Association of Social Workers, whose National Task Force on Lesbian and Gay Issues (founded in 1979 by Bernice Goodman and Ken Eisenberger) has brought enlightenment and solace to many. **Pictured below is Larry Davis, a St. Louis social worker** who specializes in the rights and problems of homosexuals in his community. Larry was co-chairperson of the NASW Task Force from 1979 to 1982.

"**R**eason has always been an intruder in the area of sexual prejudice," says **Kate Millett** in her book *Sexual Politics*. This landmark work, exploring the historical as well as contemporary issues of feminism and patriarchal oppression, brought her national attention when it was published in 1970, and the term *sexual politics* became a household phrase.

Kate is the author of several other books (including *Flying, Sita, The Prostitution Papers, The Basement,* and *Going to Iran*) and is a recognized sculptor and photographer.

Understanding early what the gay and lesbian movement would come to learn in time, Kate saw that the personal *is* the political.

She is **photographed here in her New York City studio.**

he press called it "White Night" and "A Night of Gay Rage." On May 21, 1979, former Supervisor Dan White was found guilty of manslaughter and not murder for the assassination six months earlier of openly gay Supervisor Harvey Milk and Mayor George Moscone in San Francisco's City Hall. The maximum sentence was eight years in prison. (It was not known at the time that he would be released on parole just five years later, in 1984!)

Stunned by the news, an estimated five thousand people protested the verdict outside City Hall. Combusting just one month shy of the tenth anniversary of the famous Stonewall revolt of 1969, this protest turned into a full-scale riot. San Francisco's night of gay rage shocked the nation, and proved once and for all that the gay community—at least in this city—would no longer take blatant injustice lying down.

**Pictured here is Randy Shilts, author of *The Mayor of Castro Street: The Life and Times of Harvey Milk*. Shilts, a reporter for the *San Francisco Chronicle* and formerly an anchorman for the KQED-TV *Nightly News,* stands in front of San Francisco's City Hall.**

The nation blessed above all nations is she in whom the civic genius of the people does the saving day by day in acts without external picturesqueness . . . by the people knowing their true men when they see them and preferring them as leaders to rabid partisans or empty cracks." So wrote psychologist William James.

As leaders and pioneers of the gay cause in this country, **Chuck Rowland (left) and Henry Hay (right, pictured here in front of several other heroes) co-founded the Mattachine Society in 1950.** (An original prospectus was written as early as August 1948.) The group took its name from the Société Mattachine, a secret fraternity of the French Renaissance period, the members of which were unmarried men who never appeared in public unmasked. These townsmen conducted dances and rituals during the Feast of the Fools at the vernal equinox. As Hay explains, "Sometimes these dance rituals, or masques, were peasant protests against oppression. So we took the name Mattachine because we felt that we 1950s gays were also a masked people, unknown and anonymous, who might become engaged in morale building and helping ourselves and others, through struggle, to move toward *total* redress and change."

Another 1950s homosexual organization was called ONE, Inc., founded October 15, 1952. Embracing both lesbians and gay men, ONE's purposes were four-fold: education, social service, research, and publicity. Among its long line of periodicals and other literature was the monthly *ONE Magazine*, published 1953 through 1967.

The Daughters of Bilitis, the earliest Lesbian emancipation organization in America, was founded in September 1955 by Phyllis Lyon and Del Martin.

While gay liberation did not become a public issue until the Stonewall riots of 1969, the seeds of the movement were certainly planted by these early groups. As author Marcus Overseth has written, "Without the pioneering efforts of such organizations, much of the homosexual ideas and literature which provided the philosophical roots would scarcely have existed."

**W**estern Gay Pride" was the theme as 25,000 spectators and participants gathered in August 1983 at the Nevada State Fairgrounds for the **Eighth Annual National Reno Gay Rodeo and County Fair**. Attendance had risen a hundredfold from the 250 who gathered for the first such rodeo in 1976.

The idea for an annual gay rodeo originated with Phil Ragsdale in 1975, and has found international reception. "Cowboys and cowgirls" arrived at the 1983 rodeo from as far away as England, Sweden, France, Germany, Switzerland, and Italy.

Attracting these travelers were such decidedly Western activities as bull riding, bareback bronc riding, calf roping, cow riding, barrel racing, a wild cow-milking contest, steer racing, and bulldogging. Men and women competed in all events equally.

**A**rmistead **Maupin** updated a nineteenth-century literary tradition when his serial, "Tales of the City," began appearing in the *San Francisco Chronicle* in 1976. Maupin's new wrinkle was simple and revolutionary: Gay and straight characters co-existed peacefully—even lovingly—within his epic urban saga about the residents of 28 Barbary Lane. Almost a million mainstream readers became engrossed in the struggles and triumphs of Michael "Mouse" Tolliver as he dealt with coming out to his parents, the Anita Bryant controversy, a brutal "fag bashing," and, eventually, the loss of a lover to AIDS.

The series was revised and collected into four Harper & Row novels—*Tales of the City* (1978), *More Tales of the City* (1980), *Further Tales of the City* (1982), and *Babycakes* (1984)—which have become gay best sellers throughout the English-speaking world. Maupin's finely drawn characters and intricate plots have earned him fans from all quarters. "I love these books," remarked Christopher Isherwood, "for much the same qualities that make me love the novels of Dickens."

Born in 1944, Maupin grew up in Raleigh, North Carolina, a great-great-grandson of that city's only Confederate general. After flunking out of law school, he did a stint in the Navy, serving in the Mediterranean and onshore in Vietnam. He moved to San Francisco in 1971.

A contributing editor of Andy Warhol's *Interview* magazine, Maupin has also written for *The New York Times*, the *Los Angeles Times*, and *California* magazine. His active public-speaking career on behalf of gay rights parallels that of his grandmother, Marguerite Smith Barton, who stumped England for the cause of woman suffrage in the years prior to World War I.

andy Burns left the Nevada reservation of his Paiute tribe in 1975 and immigrated to San Francisco—where his ancestry proved to be as much a liability as his gayness had been back home. Hoping to provide a sociocultural network for other urban Indians like himself, Randy—with the help of Barbara Cameron—formed the Gay American Indian organization in 1976.

In a city with a large population, feelings of isolation are common. When one is labeled a sexual outlaw, one's sense of alienation tends to increase. Thus, labels often serve to separate, but in this case, the proud label of Gay American Indian unites a community by providing a support network and a positive new way of looking at one another.

Pictured here in a San Francisco subway station, **Randy poses next to a larger-than-life–size advertisement carrying an image of the idealized American male.**

144

erry Herman musicals have long been synonymous with star-spangled entertainment and bevies of beautiful girls. There have been Dollys and Mames and Mabels galore, and **Jerry's 1983 production of *La Cage aux Folles* (see photo of marquee reflected on Broadway)** proved no exception. What was different about this Broadway show, of course, was that the beautiful girls were not girls at all—but guys in drag.

Based on the successful Parisian play and motion picture of the same name, the musical concerns the life of a successful middle-aged drag queen, his longtime lover, and the trouble they encounter when the lover's son (by a previous marriage) decides to wed the daughter of a public official.

The book is by Broadway's openly gay playwright Harvey Fierstein, himself a former drag queen, who says, "Critics expected freaktime. They wanted to see bitchy drag queens and ugly people they could sit and laugh at and feel superior to. But that's not the way I see homosexuals."

And that's not what Broadway saw, either. Instead, Fierstein, Herman, producer Allan Carr, and director Arthur Laurents supplied a splashy yet surprisingly tender musical which, as Harvey put it, "expresses the attitude that homosexuality is normal."

ntroducing Allen Ginsberg's book *Howl and Other Poems*, William Carlos Williams wrote: "We are blind and live our blind lives out in blindness. Poets are damned, but they are not blind. They see with the eyes of angels."

Regarded as a liberator of poetry by many, **Allen Ginsberg (pictured below and right, on the fire escape of his Lower East Side New York apartment)** gave a voice to a mute gay consciousness in his 1956 poem "Howl," and expressed the hidden truths about the lives of many of us. By seeing himself, he has been helping us see ourselves ever since.

Ginsberg, along with friends Jack Kerouac, Gregory Corso, William S. Burroughs, Herbert Huncke, Neal Cassady, and thirty-year companion Peter Orlovsky, spearheaded the Beat Generation of the 1950s. A vocal and visible poetic group in San Francisco, New York, and Tangiers, they opened the door for the Hip Generation of the sixties and, with it, an era of sexual exploration and discovery through the 1970s.

Ginsberg states that his single contribution to the gay movement has been "merely advocating frankness." He points to lawsuits surrounding the publishing of "Howl" and William Burroughs's *Naked Lunch* as breaking the back of literary censorship in this country once and for all. Such battles, such victories, liberated the word and encouraged gay consciousness to grow.

Ginsberg's other works include *Reality Sandwiches; Kaddish; Mind Breaths; Plutonium Ode; The Yage Letters* (with William Burroughs); *Composed on the Tongue; Straight Hearts' Delight: Love Poems and Selected Letters* (with Peter Orlovsky); and *Collected Poems (1947–1980)*.

ainstream society's idealization of masculinity—and its trappings of privilege, power, and superiority, coupled with the denigration of female characteristics as weak, dependent, and powerless—is sometimes reflected in the gay community.

"The coercion to behave like a member of one's own sex," said Margaret Mead in *Sex and Temperament in Three Primitive Societies*, "becomes one of the strongest implements with which the society attempts to mould the growing child into accepted forms . . . Every time the point of sex-conformity is made. Every time the child's sex is invoked as the reason why it should prefer trousers to petticoats, baseball-bats to dolls, fisticuffs to tears, there is planted in the child's mind a fear that, indeed, in spite of anatomical evidence to the contrary, it may not really belong to its own sex at all."

**In West Hollywood, California, machismo is not just an attitude, but a gay boutique** on Santa Monica Boulevard. Photographed during the 1982 Gay Pride Parade, police—who once arrested gays as a matter of course—lead this annual parade to symbolize our liberation.

149

**G**ay American Indian president Erna Pahe (at right) stands before the American Indian Center in San Francisco. She also stands as a symbol of hope to all lesbians and gay men facing themselves and an often uncivilized society.

"One can only face in others what one can face in oneself," writes James Baldwin in *Nobody Knows My Name*. "On this confrontation depends the measure of our wisdom and compassion. This energy is all that one finds in the rubble of vanished civilizations, and the only hope of ours."

Pushing her daughter Shannon (photo above) in a park swing, Erna makes visible the variety of roles that define her: Indian, woman, lesbian, mother, and most of all, individual.

**M**ovies can only reflect what we see in society," says **Vito Russo (below), author of _The Celluloid Closet_.** "The people who complain that movies don't reflect their lifestyles are the same people who are in the closet, and their lives are not widely visible in society. On the other hand, even if they were widely visible—as Chicanos, Blacks, and other Third World people are—I still don't think Hollywood would reflect the reality of their existence, because Hollywood is in the business of creating illusion."

One of the few filmmakers to leave the "celluloid closet" is **activist-photographer-filmmaker Pat Rocco (at left, in his Hollywood home).**

Parker Tyler, in his book _Screening the Sexes_, says, "The emergence of sexual freedom in the medium of the movies seems to me tremendously important. If the mere 'facts of life' were ever enough, mankind would always have been wisely tolerant and liberal! But the facts of life have always been moralized, penalized, arbitrarily damned and exalted, and in general hemmed in, distorted, and regimented by public institutions and official codes."

hanging the laws," according to *California Business* magazine, "does not necessarily change people's minds." **Connie O'Connor (pictured here), a nine-year veteran of San Francisco's Sheriff's Department,** might disagree. Promoted to the rank of lieutenant in 1983, she became the highest-ranking openly lesbian officer to serve on any law enforcement agency in the country. Active in the local gay community, Connie has served as president of the Alice B. Toklas Democratic Club in San Francisco (1981–1983), and makes a conscious effort to promote a positive visibility, both personally and professionally.

In a relatively short period of time, the agents of law enforcement have altered their role as oppressor of gay rights to that of protector. This dramatic shift in attitude is clearly a result of the power that visibility has to "change people's minds."

As a result of her willingness to expose a personal injustice, Sheriff O'Connor, as a visible role model, symbolizes this radical and positive change taking place in our society.

learly, there is a gay culture, even though it is rarely acknowledged by the mass media," says Peter Frisch, publisher of perhaps the country's best-known gay newspaper, *The Advocate*.

Helping to compensate for the lack of gay news in the mainstream press are publications like the one in Philadelphia called—what else?—**Gay News (see photo, right).** Other prominent newspapers include *Aloha Times* (Hawaii), *Amazon Spirit* (Montana and Idaho), *Free Spirit* (Arizona), *Gaze* (Tennessee), *Impact* (Louisiana), *Klondyke Kontact* (Alaska), *The Leaping Lesbian* (Michigan), *Mainely Gay* (Maine), *The Open Door* (Utah), *The Scene* (Colorado), *Our Time* (Oklahoma), and *Vegas Gay Times* (Nevada).

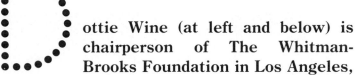

**D**ottie Wine (at left and below) is chairperson of The Whitman-Brooks Foundation in Los Angeles, the only co-sexual gay organization in the country not associated with a specific discipline. Named for gay poet Walt Whitman and lesbian painter Romaine Brooks, Whitman-Brooks promotes the development of a positive gay and lesbian identity through conferences, workshops, and rap groups.

"Though they were initially lumped together as part of the 'gay rights' movement, homosexual men and women have gradually sought separate identities. Note the now-common phrase 'gay men and lesbians,' which recognizes that gender indeed makes a significant difference, even if both sexes suffer a similarly oppressed, marginal status," states WB member Michele Kort.

In describing herself, Dottie explains, "It is all right that my 'image' may get 'tarnished' or have to be reevaluated—both by me and by my peers. I can handle others knowing that I am not 'superwoman.' As I let myself be more *vulnerable* to my lifemate, Ivy Bottini, and to loving, caring, honest, supportive peers-becoming-friends, I'm finding that it was probably only *me* that ever expected that of me anyway!

"The costs—emotionally, mentally, physically, spiritually—of the isolation of *being an image* rather than being a person are very high."

In addition to Dottie's activities with Whitman-Brooks, with which she has been affiliated since 1975, she has been on the board of directors of the Los Angeles Feminist Federal Credit Union and has served as a treasurer of the local NOW chapter.

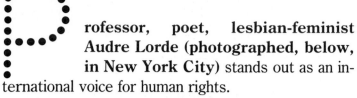

**P**rofessor, poet, lesbian-feminist Audre Lorde (photographed, below, in New York City) stands out as an international voice for human rights.

Representing the National Coalition of Black Lesbians and Gays at the twentieth anniversary in 1983 of the 1963 Civil Rights March on the nation's

capital, she became the first person to speak out for blacks and gays together before a national audience.

A professor of English and poetry at Hunter College in New York, Audre is pictured, overleaf, seated in one of the classrooms at Hunter High School, which she attended and which she remembers in her 1982 book, *Zami: A New Spelling of My Name*:

"I remember how being young and Black and gay and lonely felt. A lot of it was fine, feeling I had the

truth and the light and the key, but a lot of it was purely hell.

"There were no mothers, no sisters, no heroes. We had to do it alone, like our sister Amazons, the riders on the loneliest outposts of the kingdom of Dahomey. We were young and Black and fine and gay, sweated out our first heartbreaks with no school nor office chums to share that confidence over lunch hour. Just as there were no rings to make tangible the reason for our happy secret smiles, there were no names nor reason given or shared for the tears that messed up lab reports or the library bills.

"We were good listeners, and never asked for double dates, *but didn't we know the rules*? Why did we always seem to think friendships between women were important enough to *care* about? Always we moved in a necessary remoteness that made 'What did you do this weekend?' seem like an impertinent question. We discovered and explored our attention to women alone, sometimes in secret, sometimes in defiance, sometimes in little pockets that almost touched ('Why are those little Black girls always either whispering together or fighting?') but always alone, against a greater aloneness. We did it cold turkey, and although it resulted in some pretty imaginative tough women when we survived, too many of us did not survive at all."

Audre's third book of poetry, *From a Land Where Other People Live*, was nominated for the National Book Award in 1974, and her prose work *The Cancer Journals* received a 1981 Book Award from the American Library Association Gay Caucus.

ortrait artist **Don Bachardy (at left)** becomes the sitter in his Santa Monica, California, studio.

Bachardy's acrylic paintings of the famous and the not-so-famous have appeared in galleries around the country over the past twenty years. In 1983, *One Hundred Drawings*, a collection of portraits of literary and entertainment celebrities was published. Drawings of his companion of thirty years, Christopher Isherwood, appear on the cover of many of Isherwood's books as well.

In a 1984 interview with Mark Thompson of *The Advocate*, Bachardy, when asked about his view of the gay movement, commented, "I do feel a certain responsibility to *not* spend all of my time with my own kind. Because I do feel that one should expose oneself to heterosexuals, for one's own benefit and for theirs. I think it's very important for us to carry our message! I think it helps the cause to create a positive image."

**T**aking off the mask" was the expression used prior to "coming out of the closet" to describe the act of revealing one's sexual identity. Now, ironically, on Halloween night, the unofficial gay holiday, the masks go back on, but this time not to hide but to express—to express the joy of being different and *not* having to wear the false face of conformity in our everyday lives.

**Halloween revelers pictured here are Snow White and the Dwarves (left) in Häagen-Dazs on Castro Street in San Francisco in 1983; and a typical Halloween in Hollywood (overleaf) in 1982.**

Anita Bryant was probably visualizing a scene something like this when she said, in a 1978 *Playboy* interview: "Why do you think the homosexuals are called fruits? It's because they eat the forbidden fruit of the tree of life. God referred to men as trees, and because the homosexuals eat the forbidden fruit, which is the male sperm . . . There is even a jockey short called Forbidden Fruit. Very subtle. Did you know that?"

**C**hicago's William Kelley (photographed here in "Bughouse Square," the site on which the Windy City's first Gay Pride Parade began in 1970) has been active in the local and national gay rights movement since 1965. As his friend Barbara Gittings admits, "It never occurred to us in those early days that we could speak for ourselves." But Bill has made up for it: In 1974 he co-founded Chicago's first gay newspaper, the *Chicago Gay Crusader.*

Currently responsible for operations of *Gaylife* newspaper, Kelley says, "Social reform may sometimes be slow in coming to Chicago, but when it happens here its impact is greater on much of America than anything happening on either coast. Working for social change in the heartland is challenging."

By 1984, openly gay public and political figures were no longer complete anomalies, offering something of a new pair of glasses to the proverbially myopic public eye.

At least ninety political groups were active in this country, and a sizable handful of gay elected officials were proving that they could be both proud homosexuals and responsible Americans.

In recent years, there have been openly gay mayors in California, Florida, and Missouri; gay lawmakers in the state legislatures; gay representatives in Congress; and even a gay Human Services Director in the White House.

Financing many gay and non-gay candidates are community support groups, the largest of which is MECLA—the Municipal Elections Committee of Los Angeles. (At right: **Hollywood's Palladium marquee heralds MECLA's 1983 Human Rights Awards Banquet,** which honored such friends as Bella Abzug, Norman Lear, and guest speaker United States Senator Gary Hart.)

If MECLA is the country's premier gay fund-raising organization, then Sheldon Andelson, a board member, is most likely the country's most powerful gay man. As an attorney, Democratic party power broker, bank board chair, University of California regent, and gay activist, he once said, "Sexual preference is relevant to intimate personal relationships, but it's not relevant to anything else. By the end of the '80s, I would like to see being gay become a nonissue. That's what I see as the purpose of the movement: assimilation."

While some might disagree with this, none would dispute that his appointment to the University of California Board of Regents by Governor Jerry Brown was a milestone for the gay community.

The issue of gay rights—until recently not even an issue—has become a topic of open discussion for all politicians, gay and non-gay alike. In 1980, fifty-five members of the House of Representatives sponsored a national gay civil rights bill, and of the fifty-three that ran for reelection, fifty-one were returned to Congress. Sponsorship of the bill proved not to be the kiss of death.

f you can't raise consciousness, at least raise hell!" says **Rita Mae Brown (pictured at right in New York's Central Park)**.

For a woman with an "out"-rageous reputation, who says she never takes herself seriously, Rita has gained a reputation as a talent and a force to be taken very seriously. Not surprisingly, she has managed to raise both consciousness and hell in a world in which few of us are willing—or able—to do either. She is the author of the classic *Rubyfruit Jungle*, the story of a proud young girl growing up gay, as well as *Six of One, Southern Discomfort*, and *Sudden Death*, and numerous television and film productions.

Known and respected not only as a novelist, poet, and lecturer, but also as a founding mother of both the feminist and gay movements, Rita once said, "We have mountains to move, and we have, today, only our hands to move them with. But every day there are more hands."

n the darkness, behind closed doors, gay bars were the first social meeting places, the first "support systems" that allowed gays to congregate and socialize.

**Sapphos women's bar (right) in Seattle, Washington,** takes its name from a proud lesbian heritage: Sappho was a celebrated Greek poet who lived on the Aegean island of Lesbos off the coast of Asia Minor. Much of her poetry concerned love between women, especially her love for the girls she taught at a seventh-century B.C. "finishing school" on the island. The word *lesbian* is derived from this and, like the more generic term *homosexual*, came into popular use in the late nineteenth century. Until recently, however, *lesbian* has often been used as a

term of contempt. (A prominent politician once helped himself win an election by spreading rumors that his female opponent was a "thespian.") Today, within the lesbian community, women are proud of the label and, in fact, usually prefer it to *gay* or *homosexual*, which have become male-identified terms.

**The Closet (right)** is a mixed bar on Chicago's North Shore, attracting both males and females. Its rather ironic name is a flashback to preliberation days, when the term *the closet* was used to describe most gay life-styles: private, secretive, clandestine. Conversely, the term *coming out of the closet*, which came into popular use in the 1960s, signified an end to hiding (including from oneself) and a start of gay pride.

**L**isa Chun (at left) is co-founder of Asian Women, an Oakland-based nonpolitical support group for lesbians formed in 1978. With a membership that stretches from Hawaii to Vermont, the group strives to provide a network of information and resources for women of all Asian backgrounds—Philippine, Japanese, Korean, Chinese, Thai, Indonesian, Vietnamese—who might not, at first pass, acknowledge any degree of kinship.

While Asian Pacifics comprise only 2 percent of America's national population, in urban areas such as Los Angeles and San Francisco the percentages are much higher. In the San Francisco-Oakland area, for example, Asian Pacifics account for approximately 23 percent of the population.

Not surprisingly, the gays and lesbians within these Asian communities are banding together to form support groups of their own. Asian Pacific Lesbians and Gays (A/PLG) has been organized in Los Angeles, and the Association of Lesbian and Gay Asians (ALGA) in San Francisco.

Says Lisa: "Identity, visibility and unity need to be established. Within the past few years there have been marked divisions in the Asian lesbian community that have been very destructive. We don't seem to acknowledge each individual's viewpoints. In any movement or struggle there will always be conflicts. If we could develop a shared and mutual respect for each other's philosophies, it would show a positive forward step toward unity."

**D**avid Kopay scored a touchdown for freedom in 1975 when he publicly declared his homosexuality. A ten-year veteran of the National Football League (and former player for the Washington Redskins, San Francisco '49ers, Detroit Lions, New Orleans Saints, and Green Bay Packers), Dave tackled the American consciousness on its own playing field.

Now, nearly a decade later, David continues to exercise not only his body (see photo left, taken at David's neighborhood gym, and overleaf, on a Southern California beach) but also his rights. "I think a healthy body is one of the keys to a genuine happiness . . . and for me that health and happiness came only when I faced up to the truth of who I am."

In a speech delivered to the American Pediatrics Association in San Francisco in 1983, David said, "Those who still ask 'why do you have to talk about it?' are simply blind to the facts of life. Women are no longer being hanged as witches in this country. Blacks are no longer being lynched in the South. But right now, today, homosexuals are still beaten and often killed for no other reason than that they are gay.

"I have come to look on my mailbox as a kind of mirror of America. Ninety-five percent of the several thousand letters I've received have been positive and

supporting. . . . But the others tell me I have to keep talking, because there are people out there who would like to see us dead.

"One of my favorite letters came from a young man in Delaware. He wrote 'My life had been torture until I saw the articles about you. I thought I was losing my mind or something. When I looked at what people told me were homosexuals, I thought I'd be sick to my stomach. I've always kept everything I've felt to myself. Man, when I think what a long, cruel joke it's been, I want to go out and cream somebody. . . .'

"I can certainly sympathize with that fellow's feelings. And I've felt that way many times myself. But I learned a long time ago that going out and creaming somebody isn't going to hurt anybody but myself. You have to make peace with yourself before you can ever deal with the rest of the world.

"It's been a long and difficult journey for me to get this far. But I tell you one thing: I've never regretted being open about my homosexuality. And I have a peace of mind now I never knew before."

"One man with courage makes a majority," claimed Andrew Jackson. I would only add that one woman with courage makes a majority of men in this country nervous. And, if that woman or man is gay *and* courageous, that makes history.

One step at a time, gay men and lesbians are collectively looking forward to a positive future. We've taken a critical look at our past, and are committed never to repeat it.

More than one hundred years ago, philosopher John Stuart Mill, in his essay *On Liberty*, wrote: "Mankind speedily become unable to conceive diversity, when they have been for some time unaccustomed to see it."

Only in the last few of those hundred years have we had the courage to open wide our eyes and see all that we can imagine. We've dared to imagine breaking all of the social and psychological chains that make us "sexual slaves," and in the process a limitless range and variety of love and sexual expression has been exposed.

Making ourselves visible as gay men and lesbians is a personal, as well as political, act of love—self love. By this act we make it possible for others to see us and know us, and to join us on our road to creating not a gay nation, not a lesbian nation, but a liberated nation.

**(The photo at right was taken at the Fourth Annual West Coast Women's Music and Comedy Festival, held in Santa Barbara, California, in 1983.)**

tephen Stewart, a native of Los Angeles, set out in 1982 across this land of the free and home of the brave homosexual, in search of "the Gay American Dream."

Coming out of the closet professionally, Stephen has joined the gay men and lesbians who are daring to dream of a new and positive image of themselves. And until being gay is irrelevant to one's occupational goals and status, he intends to wear his badge of sexuality on his sleeve.

His photographs have appeared regularly since 1982 in *The Advocate*, the national gay newsmagazine, and were exhibited in 1983 at the National Gay Archives. PHOTO CREDIT: DAVID MICKELSON

# ACKNOWLEDGMENTS

A picture is often "worth a thousand words"—unless you happen to be looking at it with your eyes closed. Until I met Jim Kepner, founder and curator of the National Gay Archives in Los Angeles, that is how I looked at many of my own pictures, although I did not realize it at the time. Jim, more than any other single individual, opened my eyes to a historical perspective I could not see. Without his dedication to preserving and sharing our gay and lesbian past, envisioning a positive future would be only a dream. Without his enormous energy and eye for detail, my dream would have been only a fantasy.

One of the first photographs I took for this book captured a billboard shouting LIBERATION from the rooftop of a home near downtown Los Angeles. I passed this house each morning on my way to work for months before the ironic position of this particular message appeared, capturing my eye and my imagination. A year later, while exhibiting this and other photographs at the archives, I learned from Jim that this house was the original location of the Los Angeles Gay and Lesbian Community Services Center. The first center of its kind in this country, it served as the prototype for numerous others that would appear from coast to coast in the next decade.

Before meeting Jim Kepner, my primary connection with the gay and lesbian movement came from *The Advocate*. I picked up my first copy in the early 1970s, and by the early 1980s I was working regularly for this national gay newsmagazine as a freelance photographer. Art Director Ray Larson and former Los Angeles Editor Scott Anderson gave me the opportunity to photograph some of the images for this book.

I would like to thank the following individuals, each of whom helped tremendously to focus this documentation: my editor, Jim Landis, for being a true "frontrunner"; Sherry Robb and Bart Andrews, for sharing my vision; Barbara Romo-Farley, for pointing me in the right direction; Bette Siegel, for raising my consciousness and introducing me to Holly Near's music; Stephen Desjardins, for seeing me through it; Steven Semas, for reminding me that "to believe is to see"; my mother, Pat Gutierrez, and Frank Gutierrez, for their unconditional support; Tom Watson, for editing the text with a critical eye; Jean Pritchard, for helping me print the final images with skill; and for their assistance and support: Georgene Rada, Ed Pieczenick, Sandra Sparacio, Isabel Campo, Hortensia Amaro, Louis Jacinto, Roz Mickelson, Jim Thomas, Larry Davis, Barbara Gittings, Brian Mc-Naught, Perry Watkins, Randy Burns, David Goodstein, Ivy Bottini, Dottie Wine, Morris Kight, Fritz Heaton, Les Milne, and "the writers"—the gay and lesbian storytellers who helped me to see with depth and perspective and allowed me to tell my own story.

And finally, a word of thanks to the hundreds of gay men and lesbians, many not included in this book, who shared their struggles, hopes, and homes with me as I traveled around the country between 1982 and 1984. This book is a reflection of their collaboration and positive gay spirit.